Go-Karts

By Jeff Savage

CAPSTONE
HIGH-INTEREST
BOOKS

an imprint of Capstone Press
Mankato, Minnesota

Capstone High-Interest Books are published by Capstone Press
151 Good Counsel Drive, P.O. Box 669, Mankato, Minnesota 56002.
http://www.capstone-press.com

Library of Congress Cataloging-in-Publication Data
Savage, Jeff, 1961–
    Go-Karts/by Jeff Savage.
    p. cm.—(Wild rides!)
    Summary: Provides an overview of the history and development of
go-karts, their main features, and go-kart competitions.
    Includes bibliographical references and index.
    ISBN 0-7368-1517-1 (hardcover)
    1. Karts (Midget cars)—Juvenile literature. [1. Karts (Midget cars)
2. Karting.] I. Title. II. Series.
TL236.5 .S28 2003
796.7'6—dc21   2002012650

**Capstone Press thanks Rhonda Mims-Brown for her help in preparing
this book. Capstone Press also thanks the International Kart Federation
for their assistance.**

Editorial Credits
Matt Doeden, editor; Karen Risch, product planning editor; Kia Adams,
    series designer; Gene Bentdahl and Molly Nei, book designers;
    Jo Miller, photo researcher

Photo Credits
Corbis/Bettmann, 10, 12 (top)
Getty Images/Jonathan Ferrey, 18–19, 28; Mike Cooper, 22
Jayne Oncea, cover, 4, 7, 8, 12 (bottom), 14–15, 17, 20, 24–25, 26

1 2 3 4 5 6 08 07 06 05 04 03

Table of Contents

Learn about:

- Go-kart manufacturers

- Kinds of go-karts

- Cost of go-karts

CHAPTER 1

Go-Karts

Sixteen go-karts roll slowly toward the starting line. The drivers grip their steering wheels as they wait for the signal. The flagman waves the green flag to start the race.

The drivers press down on their gas pedals. The go-karts quickly speed up to about 70 miles (113 kilometers) per hour. The drivers enter the track's first turn. Several karts bump against one another. They slide into hay bales that sit along the edge of the track.

The rest of the karts speed toward the second turn. The drivers step on their brakes as they steer their karts into the turn. One kart stalls. It rolls to a stop. The rest of the drivers complete the turn and race down the long straightaway. They have completed one lap. They have 14 laps to go.

About Go-Karts

Go-karts are small, motorized vehicles designed to race on tracks. Most go-karts are between 4 and 6 feet (1.2 and 1.8 meters) long. Drivers sit about 1 inch (2.5 centimeters) above the ground.

People of all ages race go-karts. Children ages 8 and older participate in official go-kart events. Younger children sometimes ride for fun.

Companies in countries around the world build go-karts. Among the top go-kart builders in the United States are Track Magic, Emmick, Margay, and Invader. Many companies in Italy also build karts. These companies include Birel, Top Kart, MBA, and Tony Kart.

Types of Go-Karts

The two main types of go-karts are shifter karts and clutch karts. Shifter karts have five or six gears. Many high-performance go-karts are shifter karts. Clutch karts have just one gear. Drivers use only gas and brake pedals to speed up and slow down.

The cost of a go-kart varies. Basic karts with small engines may cost $2,000 or less. Mid-level karts have larger engines and cost about $2,500. High-performance shifter karts may cost $5,000 or more. Top racers change their go-karts to meet their racing needs. They sometimes spend more than $1,000 to set up their karts.

Go-kart drivers sit only about an inch (2.5 centimeters) off the ground.

Learn about:

- **Soapbox derby cars**

- **The first karts**

- **Early kart races**

CHAPTER 2

Early Models of Go-Karts

Modern go-karts were based on soapbox derby race cars. Soapbox derby racing began in the 1930s. Children built small race cars from large boxes that had contained soap. The children attached the boxes to roller skate wheels or wheels from baby carriages. Soapbox derby cars did not have engines. Instead, racers began at the top of a hill and coasted to the bottom.

The First Go-Karts

In 1956, mechanic Art Ingles and his friend Lou Borelli built the first modern go-kart. They attached four narrow wheels and a hand brake to a flat steel frame. They put a lawnmower engine behind the driver's seat. They called their new design a "kart."

Ingles and Borelli tested their kart in a large parking lot. Soon, a crowd of people gathered to watch the two men drive around the lot.

Go-karting grew out of the sport of soapbox derby.

People asked the men where they could find their own karts.

People quickly copied Ingles and Borelli's design. A man named Duffy Livingston started the Go-Kart Manufacturing Company. The company could not build the karts fast enough to meet the demand for them. Other companies began building karts. By 1959, 60 companies built and sold go-karts. Two years later, the number of go-kart companies in the United States had grown to more than 600.

Go-Kart Racing Begins

The sport of go-kart racing grew quickly across North America. At first, drivers held races in parking lots. Small traffic cones marked the race course. Later, courses built just for kart racing became popular. In 1957, the Go-Kart Club of America formed. This organization helped set rules for go-kart racing.

Men in the U.S. military sometimes held go-kart races at military bases in Europe. Europeans enjoyed watching the races. Go-kart racing soon spread across Europe.

Learn about:

- **Body design**

- **Tires**

- **Engine sizes**

CHAPTER 3

Designing a Go-Kart

Go-karts have become faster and more powerful over the years. Engine size and body shape are the main features that affect a kart's speed.

People of many skill levels drive go-karts. Some beginners rent karts at racing tracks. These karts usually are inexpensive clutch shifter karts with small engines. They do not have as much power as higher quality karts. Other racers take the sport very seriously. They attend racing schools and spend thousands of dollars to build high-performance karts.

The Body

The frame of a go-kart is called the chassis. All of the kart's other parts connect to this metal frame.

The front and sides of the go-kart give the vehicle its shape. The nose piece is at the front of the kart. The two side pieces are called side pods. The piece that extends up to the steering wheel is the driver's fairing. These pieces can be

made of either plastic or a strong material called fiberglass.

Go-karts are designed to reduce air resistance and to increase speed. Air must flow easily over the nose piece. Air resistance occurs when air pushes against the nose piece as the kart travels. This force slows the kart. Nose pieces often have a rounded shape to reduce air resistance.

Go-karts have rounded nose pieces to reduce air resistance.

Tires and Brakes

Most go-kart tires are made of soft rubber. Rear tires are usually about 7 inches (18 centimeters) wide. Front tires are usually about 4 inches (10 centimeters) wide. Most go-karts race on paved courses. These karts have smooth tires called slicks. Slicks grip the surface of the road well. Karts that race on dirt tracks have tires with tread. These tires have a series of bumps and grooves that help the tire grip the uneven dirt surface.

All go-karts have rear brakes. The two main parts of the brakes are the pad and the disk. These two pieces squeeze together to slow the spinning of the rear wheels. Some high-performance go-karts also have brakes on the front wheels. This setup is called "four-wheel brakes."

On paved tracks, go-karts use smooth tires called slicks.

Engines

Go-kart engine size is measured in cubic centimeters (cc). The smallest kart engine is 50cc. These small engines are for karts designed for children as young as 5 years. A kart with a 50cc engine can reach speeds of about 35 miles (56 kilometers) per hour.

Most karts have larger engines. Clutch karts with 100cc engines can travel more

than 60 miles (97 kilometers) per hour. Karts with 125cc engines can reach speeds of more than 100 miles (160 kilometers) per hour on long tracks. The largest go-kart engines are 250cc. These engines can power a kart to more than 140 miles (225 kilometers) per hour. Only skilled drivers should attempt to race at these high speeds.

Small engines are placed at the back of a go-kart.

Learn about:

- Go-kart tracks

- Competition classes

- The World Championships

CHAPTER 4

Go-Karts in Competition

Many professional race car drivers got their start by racing go-karts. Jeff Gordon, Tony Stewart, Sam Hornish Jr., and other racing stars once raced go-karts. They learned basic auto racing skills in these races. Some professional drivers continue to race go-karts during their off-season to keep their racing skills sharp.

Speedway tracks are oval-shaped. They usually include two long turns.

Go-Kart Tracks

Go-kart tracks are common across North America and Europe. Many tracks are privately owned. Drivers pay track owners for the use of their tracks. Other tracks are owned by clubs. Club members pay dues to use the tracks.

The three main types of go-kart tracks are sprint tracks, speedway tracks, and road race tracks. Sprint tracks are paved, curvy tracks. They are usually between 1,300 feet (400 meters) and 4,000 feet (1,200 meters) long.

Speedway tracks are also called ovals. They have two long straightaways with a long curve at each end. Most speedways are dirt tracks, but some are paved. Speedways are usually one-eighth mile (201 meters) long.

Road race tracks are paved tracks that are also used in races for larger cars. They usually have many twists and turns. Most road race tracks are between 1.5 miles (2.4 kilometers) and 3 miles (4.8 kilometers) long.

Racing Classes

Go-kart racers are divided into classes. Classes are separated by age, engine size, and weight. Drivers only compete against drivers of a similar age with similar karts and engines. These classes keep each race fair.

A go-kart and its driver must meet a minimum weight requirement before a race. Any kart that does not meet the minimum

weight must have weight added before the race. Five-pound (2.3-kilogram) lead weights are added to the kart. For example, in a 250-pound (113-kilogram) weight class, if the kart and driver weigh only 240 pounds (109 kilograms), two weights must be added. The weights are attached to the back and sides of the driver's seat.

Racing classes help officials make sure all drivers and karts in a race are about equal.

Helmets, gloves, and other safety gear keep go-kart drivers safe.

Racing Events

In the United States, two go-kart organizations hold most official go-kart races. They are the International Kart Federation (IKF) and

the World Karting Association (WKA). The IKF holds most of its races in the western part of the United States. The WKA holds most races in the east.

Each organization holds championships each year. Sometimes, drivers must win smaller races before they can compete in the championships. A European organization called Commission International de Karting (CIK) holds the World Championships. As many as 40,000 fans attend this event each year.

Safety

Go-kart drivers always keep safety in mind. They wear helmets with face shields. They also wear gloves, high-top shoes or boots, and special driving suits that do not rip easily.

Go-kart tracks are also built to be safe. Track designers make sure no trees, fences, or other objects are too close to a course. Track officials must place hay bales, tires, or other barriers around any objects that a racer could hit. These safety practices help keep go-kart racing safe and fun.

Jeff Gordon

Jeff Gordon is one of the most successful race car drivers in the world. Today, he races stock cars on NASCAR's Winston Cup series. But he was once a successful go-kart driver. Gordon learned many of the skills he uses in NASCAR races today by racing go-karts.

Gordon was born August 4, 1971, in Vallejo, California. At age 5, he started driving go-karts for fun. By age 9, he was taking part in and winning organized go-kart races. He often competed against much older drivers. At age 10, Gordon drove in 25 go-kart races. He won all of them.

Gordon began driving stock cars in 1993. Two years later, he won his first Winston Cup championship. He also won Winston Cup titles in 1997, 1998, and 2001.

Words to Know

air resistance (AIR ri-ZISS-tuhnss)—the force of air that pushes against and slows down moving objects

chassis (CHASS-ee)—the frame on which the body of a vehicle is built

fiberglass (FYE-bur-glass)—a strong, lightweight material made from thin threads of glass

slicks (SLIKS)—smooth tires often used to race on paved surfaces

tread (TRED)—a series of bumps and deep grooves on a tire; tread helps tires grip uneven surfaces.

To Learn More

Martin, Gary. *Go Kart Racing—Just for Kids: A Step by Step Guide to Go Kart Racing.* Ft. Wayne, Ind.: Martin Motorsports, 2000.

Smith, Jay H. *Kart Racing.* Motorsports. Mankato, Minn.: Capstone Press, 1995.

Useful Addresses

International Kart Federation
1609 South Grove Avenue
Suite 105
Ontario, CA 91761

Superkarts! USA
6365 Old Avery Road
Suite 6
Dublin, OH 43016

World Karting Association
6051 Victory Lane
Concord, NC 28027

Internet Sites

Track down many sites about Go-Karts.
Visit the FACT HOUND at *http://www.facthound.com*

IT IS EASY! IT IS FUN!

1) Go to *http://www.facthound.com*
2) Type in: 0736815171
3) Click on "FETCH IT" and FACT HOUND will find
   several links hand-picked by our editors.

Relax and let our pal FACT HOUND do the research for you!

Index